POETRY OF EVERYTHING

STRANDS OF POEMS ON LOVE, LIFE AND BEYOND

HARSH SHARMA

To art.

To you.

To nothing.

To everything.

Contents

Contents

Preface

"Book, book, book,

   O pretty tiny book!

   Thou is life,

   and life is thee.

   Bless the hands holding thee.

   Bless the eyes beholding thee.

   Bless thy reader with thy words,

   with thy pages, with thy glee."

-Harsh

If feeling were a body, the poems residing in "The Poetry Of Everything" would have been nerves; nerves of ecstasy and sorrow and melancholy and hope. Ranging from introversion which is the author's favorite spot to be on, this book goes to exploring mankind at its best, at its worst, and in between. Harsh has inhaled what air around him brought him and breathed out poetry; readable or not, it's in your hands.

Acknowledgements

> *"Thank you, thank you,*
> *Thank you universe!*
> *Thank you boons,*
> *And thank you curse!*
> *Thank you grey of life,*
> *And the colors so diverse!*
> *Thank you pen, paper,*
> *poetry, and verse."*

-Harsh

Primarily, I bow in front of my maker to bless me with the art of communicating my thoughts on paper. My life was not meaningful if I were not writing!

My selfish hands reach to the feet of my loving mother and sacrificial father. I was a scribbler. Your support raised a writer.

Then let me be grateful for the good and bad circumstances which created much-needed whirlpools in my mind.

I'm sending love and only love to you, yes you, to pick up this book. Come, let me kiss your hands!

A bouquet of gratitude to the exceptional team at Notion Press. Your tools and work of perfection are all that a budding author craves.

ACKNOWLEDGEMENTS

Thank you pexels.com for providing me with amazing pictures for the depiction, free of cost.

Last but not the least, a peck on the forehead and a pat on the back to the person in my mirror. Thank you for not giving up and reaching here!

1. The Quaint Writer Boy

*They assumed he had some disorder,
as he always found quaint games to play and refused to be a part
of gully cricket.*

He had powers;
Powers in his quixotic world
which were mistaken;
Mistaken for his weaknesses,
in the world, he was living in.
Cons of hallucination were told him,
every now and then,
but for him,
that dreamland had everything;
Even better!
He wrote it!
He wrote the chaos of the existing world, obnoxious to his world
of imagination.
He knew innovation on paper was his power,
and his absurdly romantic mind was his boon
until he grew up one day.
Now,
it's a beautiful curse,
as he is big now,
and the world is not yet ready,
for one like him.

2. Anything But A Writer

*"Only a writer who has the sense of evil can make
goodness readable."*

-E.M. Forster

Don't you dare tell me your story!
I'll write it to the world,
And will make it mine.
I'm a stealer,
I'm a black-legged writer.
Don't you dare scare me with a sword,
I will kill you with my pen.
And write your death a suicide.
I'm a mingy,
I'm a crime writer.
Don't you dare exaggerate your art before me,
I'll leak my pen and stigmatize it.
And write that it never existed.
I'm poison,
I'm a wicked writer.
Don't you dare tell me what to write,
I'll write what I gotta write.
I'm not hired for what you read.
I'm a whimsical,
I'm a narcissistic writer.
Don't you dare convince me to tell a lie,
I'm gonna write your ugly truths.
My nib is heedless to beautiful lies.
I'm a blunt,
I'm a satirical writer.

Heaven isn't made for me,
I would fall like November's leaves.
Don't pick me up, crush me when I die,
I'm a liar.
I'm anything but a writer.

3. After Ages Of Unlove

Oh, love,
You're spring.
My leaves are growing since you came.

And it's after ages; ages of loveless autumn.
Oh, love,
You're a rain.
My days are alive since you came.
And it's after ages; ages of barren time.
Oh, love,
You're food.
My soul is full since you came.
And it's after ages; ages of hungry forever.
Oh, love,
You're the moon.
My nights are silver since you came.
And it's after ages; ages of wicked black.
Oh, love,
You're caffeine.
My spirits are high since you came.
And it's after ages; ages of dismay.
Oh, love,
You're fireplace.
My winters are easy since you came.
And it's after ages; ages of fatal snow.
Oh, love,
You're ink.
My pen is writing since you came.
And it's after ages; ages of my blank journal.
Oh, love,
You're sugar.

My edibles are sweet since you came.
And it's after ages; ages of the insipid tongue.
Oh, love,
You're me.
I lie within me since you came.
And it's after ages; ages of lost me.
Oh, love,
You're a day-star.
Bathing naked in your light since you came.
And it's after ages; ages of an uncomfortable array.
Oh, love,
You are highway.
My journey is smooth since you came.
And it's after ages; ages of potholes.
Oh, love,
You're god.
The devotee in me is awakened since you came.
And it's after ages; ages of atheism.
Oh, love,
You're a book, a good book.
I'm in harmony with words since you came.
And it's after ages; ages of reader's block.
Oh, love,
You're impossible.
I'm living a fantasy since you came.
And it's after ages; ages of realism.

Oh, love,
You're Rockabye.
I'm having a baby sleep since you came.
And it's after ages; ages of adult nights.
Oh, love,
You're love.
My love is loved since you came.
And it's after ages; ages of unlove.

4. My Feathery Sentiments

Valves of my heart are cottony enough,
It's easy to pinch my nerve of misery.

My face won't yell that I'm hurt,
It stings inside the soul to the core.
I know I'm impossible, and even herculean to get,
But my feathery sentiments are quelled and wet.
The gardener is flowering me at my pace,
But they say blooming is vital for a flower.
I know that, and I'll bloom one day,
But for now, the torrent has withered me.
I know I'm a blossom with a churn so fat.
But my feathery sentiments are quelled and wet.
I own a swarm of emotions within,
An ocean filled with sweets and salts.
I feel too much, too much of it,
whether it's a stab or a peck on my neck.
I forgive, and don't give in to tit for tat,
But my feathery sentiments are quelled and wet.
My skin is fragile, and so is my flesh.
So are my bones, so is my blood.
So is what's beneath, my silly ass, soul.
And I know fragile doesn't mean weak, it's flexible.
They say pliable fails when life throws a net,
But my feathery sentiments are quelled and wet.
No, I'm not obscure of hurdles,
I know life is a bittersweet wine.
But for now, I want to lay down in the snow,
And wait for the sun to melt it and make me flow again.
I know it's written, destined, and all set,

But my feathery sentiments are quelled and wet.
My chest is heavy, loaded with guilt.
Or if it's not guilt, it is a heap of hurts.
Each voice of mine has its own theory to babble,
And I wonder if I am too much in my head.
Sometimes I feel I'm being a pessimistic brat,
But, you know what, it's true that my feathery sentiments are
quelled and wet.

5. Coming Of Age

"They say during puberty you're like a book with empty pages, ready to be written. Though you're much more of an empty bookshelf within a burning library."

-Jonathan Purol

I will find love, and love will find me.
I'll cross paths with a doppelganger vibe.
I'll meet people, weirdly awesome and awesomely weird,
I'll make my own tribe.
This is what my newly redder heart screams,
Coming of age underlays a castle of dreams.
I'll explore the roads,
and I will swim through the sea.
I'll fly the infinite sky
and have the nectar of life like a bee.
Life seems quanta of healing sunbeams.
Coming of age underlays a castle of dreams.
I want to know what a kiss feels like,
I wanna feel butterflies with a human touch.
I want to be clasped in arms with my flaws,
And a peck on the forehead, nothing much.
Inside me, a light of endorphin gleams,
Coming of age underlays a castle of dreams.
I want to hop like a squirrel on the grass,
I want to sprint like a tiger in the woods.
I want to get tickled by a race of hormones,
I want to travel the spectrum of moods.
I want to taste the blues, I want to breathe the greens.
Coming of age underlays a castle of dreams.
I want to get deceived,

I want to get hurt.
I want to fill my voids,
I want both lotus and dirt.
I want to smell maturity, I want to create scenes.
Coming of age underlays a castle of dreams.
I want reality to hit me hard,
I want to break my own heart.
I want to break down on my knees,
And then raise for a fresh start.
I want to know what life holds, and what it means.
Coming of age underlays a castle of dreams.

6. Oh, Not You!

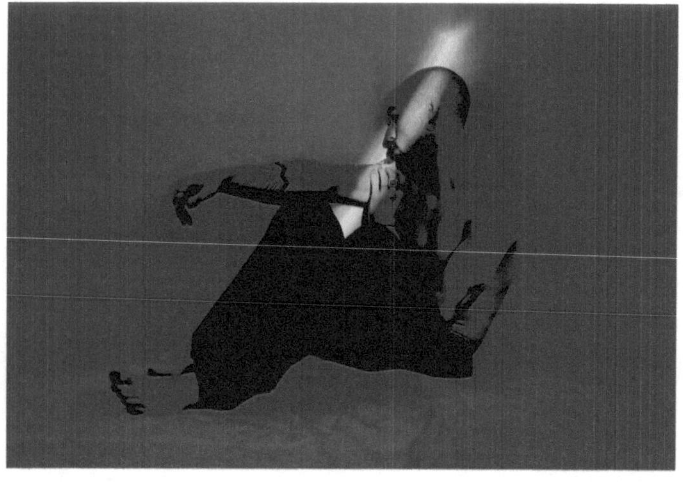

It's raining cats and dogs outside,
And the sprinkles of it reminisce of you.
Walkin' down the memory aisle,
I see you getting doused with me.

But as stops the downpour, so do you.
I'm drenched now, oh, not you!
It's scorching sun making my pores leak,
And the rays of it reminisce of you.
Walkin' down the memory aisle,
I see you under an umbrella with me.
But as cools down the sun, so do you.
I'm tanned now, oh, not you!
It's a jam-packed road and I'm stuck,
A clutter of horns reminisces of you.
Walkin' down the memory aisle,
I see you napping a bit with me.
But as cuts the jam, so do you.
I'm sleeping now, oh, not you!
It's a moonless light painting the sky black,
And the blackness of it reminisces of you.
Walkin' down the memory aisle,
I see you, the moon, hands in hands with me.
But as vanishes the gloom, so do you.
I'm black now, oh, not you!
It's the air of love roaming around the town,
And the pinkness of it reminisces of you.
Walkin' down the memory aisle,
I see you making love with me.
But as fleets Euphoria, so do you.
I'm dry of love now, oh, not you!
It's the debt of nature knocking on my door,

The harshness of it reminisces of you.
Walkin' down the memory aisle,
I see you promising forever with me.
But as unties my soul, so do you.
I'm dead now, oh, not you!

7. If I Die In Jasmine's Shadow

If I say I love roses,
Would you walk me to the rose garden?

If I say they won't get it,
Would you say, "Come, baby, let's run?"
If I say my feet are fragile,
Would you hold me in your arms?
If I say let's sleep under stars,
In the moonlight, would you praise my charms?
Would you say my face is divine,
though I have an ugly scar?
Would you drive me to the shore of the city,
Holding my hand in your car?
If I say, let's love in this moment,
Would you cuddle me under these skies?
If I say it's darkest over here,
Would you bring me fireflies?
If I die in jasmine's shadow,
Would you, my darling, those moments, miss?
And then nearing a lifeless me,
On my shut eyes, would you plant a kiss?

8. Oh, Dear Woman!

Oh, dear Woman!
You give life out of you,
Tend to nurture it at the same time.
You feel all the beautiful pains,
And know how to blush at the same time.
You're a delicate and fragile flower,
And furious fire at the same time.
You are a mother, a sister, a friend, a wife,
And you are 'you' too at the same time.
The beauty of your soothing scars,
The ignition of your bright eyes,
The roughness of your un-tearable skin
And butter touch of it at the same time,
Is incomparably Beautiful.
And your beauty is on its peak,
When you flow like an insane breeze.
In your damn fuckin' way,
In your kind of ease!

9. Love Of An Orchid

"You need your own love to save your heart."

-Rithvik Singh

Ask for a flower,
But bloom yours first.
Get drown in Romeo's love,
But zoom yours first.

I so agree that hands are made to hold,
But when they leave, you ought to be enough bold.
Lost in the sympathetic world, you are, I know!
But avalanche is what for they hate snow.
'They' won't embrace you for what you are,
Unconditional love is the sweetest myth so far!
Though this myth is a truth when you expect from the mirror,
Cause that's the only fucking constant till demise is near.
Don't be a Rose to entertain their nostrils,
You are just perfectly gorgeous, even being orchids.
And I'm not saying you necessarily need to hate 'em,
But whites aren't always gifted,
Sometimes you have to create them.

10. The Poetry Of Fake

With a burdened chest,
Eyes full of unrest,
I'm sitting with my pen,

What to write, is a quest.
I don't want it to bleed my miseries,
Neither I want to pen my tears.
I want to write poetry of fake,
Like an angelic love among my fears.
Like how the little slum chap,
Danced in a heavy downpour.
Like parading tiny black ants,
Don't give a shit 'bout lion's roar.
Like round round jalebis in pan,
Gonna be dipped in sugar syrup.
Like soil smells during rain,
And on a cold night, you got a teacup.
Let's see, where this ink leads to,
And what fruit, my imagination breeds to.
What's sure is I'm not gonna cry,
Joy is I'm gonna fake, joy is I'm gonna try.

11. The Second Girl Child

*"A daughter is one of the most beautiful gifts this
world has to give."*

-Laurel Atherton

Again, it is an eight-month-old bulge,
It is the family's second child.
Everyone is on cloud nine,

But there's a worry, that is mild.
The first child was a delicate, little doll,
What would be second, leave it on nature's call.
Everyone is praying for it to be a boy,
But destiny isn't something, you will call a toy.
Labour pain grows and everyone joins hands,
God is buttered today with extra garlands.
And here comes the cry,
The angel is here.
Soft as cotton,
Pink and fair.
No one is disheartened,
But no one either celebrated.
'Though it would be better if it were a boy,
It's fine, we're liberated.
Both are needed, boy and girl,
What can we do if the girl was fated?
But I wonder if there were two boys,
They would have been equally charismatic toys.
Two is the problem when the gender is female,
It's the second girl child, so everyone's pale.

12. She Is My Best Friend

"My favorite journey is looking out the window."

-Edward Gorey

Warm sunlight intrudes through her,
She reflects the world outside.
Who made my favorite curry today,
To whose yard, came a new bride.
Cutting the woods from dense woods,
She was made many years ago.
Now the termites have blessed her,
With several holes for a binocular show.
Whenever it rains, I sit beside her.
Smell the soil and read beside her.
On festive occasions,
when she wears new curtains.
My mother makes sure,
she doesn't get stains.
All my fantasies, all my regrets,
My window is my best friend,
She knows all my secrets.

13. Who Is The Real Man?

"First find the man in yourself if you will inspire manliness in others."

-Amos Bronson Alcott

Getting on knees isn't your thing,
You ought to detach from vulnerabilities.
Water in your eyes makes you pussy,
And guess what, it does question your capabilities.
Walk like a cock, be like a rock,
Drain all the emotions, that's a bullshit stock.
Walk straight, talk straight, slang them 'cause you can!
Because that's what, you effeminate dog, makes you a real man.
But...
I get on knees, then rise like dust,
Being vulnerable is a humane must.
I weep my strength through my eyes,
It doesn't affect what's between my thighs.
I walk my walk, I talk my talk,
And being kind is my kind of thing.
And I do fly in the breeze of emotions,
Because, you fucking moron, I got a wing!
And if it's burning your ass to ashes,
Go get stripped under a fan.
'Cause I don't need to be fully naked,
To tell you WHO IS THE REAL MAN!

14. An Ecstatic Start To My Short Tale

"*Every great love starts with a great story.*"

-Nicholas Sparks

My eyes glistened when I peeped through the pane,
Wearing dry leaves was smiling a perpetual lane.

Its charm multiplied by times,
the moment my gaze caught him.
Crushing the leaves under his boots,
Walking to the café with charisma, not dim.
A big white canvas hung on his shoulder,
And in his hands, he got some brushes.
In the bag, there must be a crowd of paints,
And the air around him was filled with mushes.
For a fleeting moment, when my eyes met his,
I could capture the twinkle in his eyes.
It pecked my nerve of ecstasy,
causing my stomach plenty of butterflies.
He neared me, and with ease, asked, "Would you mind
giving me your place, to be a little kind?"
He wished for the window seat, to enrich his craft,
But, alas! I hadn't written yet, my very first draft.
Though the voice had hues worth falling for,
The idea of agreeing on a whim,
Would have given him a score.
So I said, "sorry, I can't,
I'm writing a story.
But to add to your painting,
a little touch of glory,
Sit beside me, and give me grass,
Would you paint me on your canvas?"
He shied, his face reddened,
absolutely right hit the nail.

And there I got as a by-product,
an ecstatic start to my short tale.

15. A Tarnished Rose

"Menstrual blood is the only source of blood that is not traumatically induced. Yet in modern society, this is the most hidden blood, the one so rarely spoken of and almost never seen, except privately by women."

-Judy Grahn

There are four days a month I bleed,
The days which gift me a voucher of cramps.
My mood goes whimsical exploring the spectrums,
Either I belong to angel house or behind the door of vamps.
One moment beautifies me, another says I am gross.
And the world calls me a tarnished rose.
The gods have locked their doors for me,
The walls of the kitchen have put a restrain.
You calling me weak and a crying baby,
Break your five bones and feel my pain.
This is my construction, not one of my flaws.
And the world calls me a tarnished rose.
If weren't your mom a bleeder,
You won't be breathing here.
The divine power of femininity it is,
Respect it, don't shame or fear.
Creation was what, for women, He chose,
And the world calls me a tarnished rose.
Once I said aloud SANITARY PADS!
Rebukes I got and I was hushed.
No, it wasn't a cuss word or slang.
It was taboo, so old and crushed.
A pad is a protector, not a venomous dose.
And the world calls me a tarnished rose.
There is at stake my capability,

As is at its worst my vulnerability.
No matter if it's my second toughest day,
I can't make nature, an excuse for my inability.
I have to keep my morale up and my tasks on the nose,
And the world calls me a tarnished rose.
Medical stores are ashamed of it,
What can we expect from the rest of the crowd?
Whenever they pack pads in black polythene,
They make sure it doesn't make a noise so loud.
They treat it as the bane of poetry or dirty prose,
And the world calls me a tarnished rose.
Pores on my skin crave pampering,
My bosom needs a bear hug.
I need love, the most of it,
not a churn or a shrug.
No, it's more than a sympathy-seeking pose!
And the world calls me a tarnished rose.
Not a hue to entertain your eyes,
I'm a blood so pretty, brown and pink.
Not an incense to serve your nostrils,
I smell like the very life, I don't stink.
A rose is a love like me, free of laws.
No, I am not a tarnished rose.

16. Not A Pseudo-Feminist

"Each time a woman stands up for herself, without knowing it possibly, without claiming it, she stands up for all women."

-Maya Angelou

No, I am not a men hater,
Don't mistake me as a predator.
My appetite is starving for equality,
And for that, I work as a navigator.
I don't give false hope, I am not a pessimist,
I am a woman who knows her esteem, not a pseudo-feminist.
No, I don't want to be a man,
Moreover, I don't want to be one.
I just want similar rights,
And with love, not on a point of a gun.
I want to bring it straight, not with a turn or twist,
I am a woman who knows her esteem, not a pseudo-feminist.
No, my aim isn't to oppress,
My aim is to raise women to equal.
I want to make my original,
Not an extended sequel.
I want my girl to make time hers, not just wear it on her wrist,
I am a woman who knows her esteem, not a pseudo-feminist.
I want to empower women for themselves,
Get it, I'm not spoiling them.
The thick robes of honor that roped us off,
I am up for uncoiling them.
The sun of freedom is needed, it's enough of slavery's mist,
I am a woman who knows her esteem, not a pseudo-feminist.
No, I don't want you to carry a child,
But you too can take care of it, can't you?
No, I don't want any special attention,

I just want to be wanted as they want you.
I am a struggler, not on your enemies' list.
I am a woman who knows her esteem, not a pseudo-feminist.
I want petals, but I want to earn them,
For that, I'm ready to walk over nails.
I know with rights, chase the responsibilities,
I want passes, I too want fails.
I want my power in my fist.
I am a woman who knows her esteem, not a pseudo-feminist.
I want to cage out,
But not on the cost of caging someone else.
I just want a gender-neutral sky,
Where everyone flies, and no one quells.
I want a healthy diet, not a toxic grist.
I am a woman who knows her esteem, not a pseudo-feminist.
No, I don't want to change something between my thighs.
Cause that is something I call a blessing.
I just want due credits for my capability,
Not a bungalow against sea-facing.
My identity is all my life's gist,
I am a woman who knows her esteem, not a pseudo-feminist.
Trust me when you will let me fly,
You too will get new wings.
Because typical manhood tortures you too,
You also want to get free of those rings.
I'm in my damn senses, don't consider it a jest.
I am a woman who knows her esteem, not a pseudo-feminist.

Not only men but there are also many women,
who have set bars for one's exemption.
The struggle is with you, the struggle is with us,
It's not a moonwalk as per your assumption.
I want fire, not to be worshipped by a priest.
I am a woman who knows her esteem, not a pseudo-feminist.

17. I Love A Love Of Another Land

"Love is never wrong."

-Melissa Etheridge

My love is not a handful of stardust,
It is more of the blood of wars.
But when our fingers intertwine,
Her touch washes all my scars.
Neither of the waters nor of the sand,
I love a love of another land.
My love is not a bed of roses,
It is a broad highway of thorns.
It is a mangled yet living cottage,
Standing between thunderous storms.
An abandoned flower from a garland,
I love a love of another land.
My love is not either violet or red,
It lies somewhere midway spectrum.
Green of grasping on a serviette of saffron
is what makes it a euphoric sum.
Eternity it is, not a fashion trend.
I love a love of another land.
No, it doesn't smell like a man.
It breathes the air of effeminacy.
Lipstick here kisses the lipstick of other,
Not a mustache of supremacy.
The world thinks my love needs mend.
I love a love of another land.
My love isn't a lullaby to your sleeping child,
It's more of a warrior's anthem.

It's seeking the throne of validation,
Don't panic, it's not a phantom.
It's not a foe of culture, it has a humane stand.
I love a love of another land.
No, my love is not a lump of clay,
You can't orient it as a child's play.
My love is like an ancient sea,
With passionate waves yet not a flea.
My love is a life, not an event grand,
I love a love of another land.
My love is not new,
It always has been there.
Some units of it got chained in marriage,
And some closeted in drawers of fear.
And honor gulped some in its esophageal gland,
I love a love of another land.
My love isn't a ravishing dress of my choice,
It is an art of the god, like my skin, and my very voice.
It is not an outcome of brainwashing,
It is as raw as a mother's labor noise.
You can't shake it off with your dirty rant.
I love a love of another land.
The soul is the lock, and love is the key,
I found mine, so you envy?
Fake is the new love for you,
And that doesn't set the lovers free.
Love is love, not a gender brand,

I love a love of another land.
My love is used to crackers of hate,
No more it steps aback with the slap of abnormality.
It is somewhere beyond the horizon,
Lighting out the gloom of culpability.
On an underrated star, am waiting for my girlfriend,
I love a love of another land.

18. Like Many In Your Vicinity

"In the race of hunger and respect, hunger won."

-Moumita Haldar

Painting her lips blood-red and loud,
Complementing them with smoky eyes.
A shimmering black dress hugs her body,
That reveals her pedicured legs and thighs.
Indispensable wants of life demolish her dignity,
She's a human, in the skin of a woman, like many in your
vicinity.
She, a lotus, emerges out of that miry brothel,
To sit with glued lips, in a glimmering grey car.
That, exploring the pathogenic streets, will drop her,
At a hotel with worn-off paint, that looks bizarre.
A wolf-cum-human waits there, for her with certainty.
She's a human, in the skin of a woman, like many in your
vicinity.
She isn't allowed to cry,
As she must look attractive.
For hungry men of the city out there,
With their sins so secretive.
She's surviving the blues, swallowing her culpability,
She's a human, in the skin of a woman, like many in your
vicinity.
As she is a pro now,
She knows all the good hacks.
The more her sling bag would load with money,
The better she would show off all her cracks.
Once what they called a red flag, was now her unwanted ability.

She's a human, in the skin of a woman, like many in your
vicinity.
But what about the cracks,
Which lies within her?
They aren't allowed to see the light,
So, she often hides them beneath a blur.
Acceptance would make it easy for her; no, it's not her imbecility.
She's a human, in the skin of a woman, like many in your
vicinity.
She knows it's just one more time,
That she would have to sell herself.
But she can buy joy for her sisters,
And fill, with books, their broken shelf.
She crushes her soft petals, to bloom their serenity.
She's a human, in the skin of a woman, like many in your
vicinity.
You must ponder why she chose this world?
It's just that her stars were not in her favor.
She was hauled into this through a racket,
Since then, her destiny owned a bitter flavor.
The more she tried to rise from the drain, the more pulled her its
gravity.
She's a human, in the skin of a woman, like many in your
vicinity.
It's not so she didn't try to escape,
But the lines on her palms were in a tangled shape.
The fine when she got caught red-handed,

Were either black and blue marks, or a relentless rape.
She still remembers when it was the first time,
The man from the politics asked for a blowjob.
She was forced onto her fragile knees,
And all her heart did was pound and throb.
The monster wore pride though he was committing infidelity,
She's a human, in the skin of a woman, like many in your
vicinity.
The chronology of life that followed was disastrous.
She doesn't fear now, and you know what, that's dangerous.
She beholds dreams now, and calls herself a lady,
And the confidence she is bathed in, you'll find it outrageous.
A mother to three orphans, and a sister to many like her,
Life tried to break her, but she wasn't made to stir.
It's high time you think highly of her, she will forgive your
audacity.
As she's a human, in the skin of a woman, like many in your
vicinity.

19. I Don't Wear It On My Sleeve

The sun might delay for your day to start,
But I have to rise up before the sun.

No matter, fever, cold, or headache,
I have to lace up and tighten my bun.
There are times when it churns me up,
But I don't wear it on my sleeve.
I love to first dish my kids platters,
But that doesn't mean I'm not famished.
Many a time, I want to cook for myself,
But I don't as you don't like garnished.
There are times when my tongue too craves,
But I don't wear it on my sleeve.
Yours were edifice, I made it home.
Not for no reason the world calls me a homemaker.
I cemented my dreams under these bricks,
How on earth would the world know me as a baker?
There are times when I want to fly,
But I don't wear it on my sleeve.
When you come home dog fatigued,
I also need to crash on the bed.
My working hours aren't nine to five,
And that's unfair, moreover, that's sad.
There are times when I want to scream like you,
But I don't wear it on my sleeve.
You say you earn bread for the family,
And that tops the works of importance.
But what if I serve you raw bread,
Would you throw away your sexist lens?
I know the home runs when we burn together,

But I don't wear it on my sleeve.
I agree you earn those pink and brown notes,
But you are a broke without my accountancy.
Never you ask where the money came from,
Whenever knocks our door an emergency.
I know my commerce is so underrated,
But I don't wear it on my sleeve.
I am a motherly mom to my angels,
I'm a daughter to your parents.
I'm a good wife, a good housewife,
And a saviour for all the torrents.
There are times when I want to be myself,
But I don't wear it on my sleeve.
No, I am not saying I need your pity,
Being a homemaker is my best ever choice.
Validation and esteem are what I seek for,
And a Sunday, free from each and every noise.
There I times when I too want to rest,
But I don't wear it on my sleeve.
You're just a slave of your rituals,
Not an antagonist in my story.
What if we become each other's helping hand,
And walk together with ravishing glory?
I too have emotions, I too have notions,
But I don't wear it on my sleeve.
I wouldn't have puked this out,
If I were a hero in your script.

I wouldn't have walked this much,
If I were allowed to use the lift.
It's today when the water went over my head,
that I had to wear it on my sleeve,
that I had to wear it on my sleeve.

20. The Mother In Me

"Biology is the least of what makes someone a mother."

-Oprah Winfrey

They said you are lesser of a woman,
Your womb can't carry a child.
My femininity, they doubted every now and then,
And societal taunts went tense from mild.
Strutting on thorns, for you, won't be steady.
As you don't own a motherly body.
What is the use of the breasts you got,
If you can't feed a human from them.
Herculean it will be to safeguard your marriage,
As reproduction is what gives it glam.
White isn't white, if doesn't get muddy,
As you don't own a motherly body.
They said you might be short of blessings,
You can't even raise your husband's lineage.
It's tough to survive behind the bars,
When jailor is the motherhood, infertility is the cage.
Abnormally, o woman, your genitals are bloody,
As you don't own a motherly body.
How would you survive the blues of senility,
Without a child, there is no good.
A life that is short would feel long enough,
Intolerant you might become, or maybe crude.
Whom would you buy barbies and a teddy,
As you don't own a motherly body.
Chewing and gulping bread of patience,

I listened to all my nears and dears.
Though I was the victim of a psychic agony,
Open, for all the comments, were my ears.
This individual lady knows how to be steady,
As the mother in me is not just a body.

Incessant was the noise,
I was waiting for them to stop.
To tell, from the hint of light in the gloom,
I find my daily dose of hope.
Pure white is as inevitable as muddy,
As the mother in me is not just a body.

I know my seed isn't capable enough,
But that's not unfortunate, that's biology.
God happened to shape my life like that,
You better understand Her chronology!
A woman isn't a woman for how much she gets bloody,
As the mother in me is not just a body.

Please, don't dishonor the word "mother,"
By terming it a connection so physical.
Mother is a water deeper than the ocean,
The way you define her is quite unradical.
Come, I would buy you barbies and a teddy,
As the mother in me is not just a body.

My blood that runs fluid of motherhood,
Is pumped by the heart that beats my womanhood.
For whomsoever I care, I cry, I fear,
Is the apple of my eye, my child, my dear.

Being unsafe myself, I give it my custody,
As the mother in me is not just a body.
So what if my breasts cannot make milk, I have sheltered many
in my bosom.
So what if the plant doesn't belong to me,
I have nurtured its leaves and its blossom.
I'm your everything, yet I am nobody.
As the mother in me is not just a body.

21. Him And Me

"*God is most glorified in us when we are most satisfied in Him.*"

-John Piper

Don't tell me He is bound to four walls,
and that He flows as does air.
Don't tell me He swims blue waters,
and sees in a compassionate stare.
What if I say, He is everywhere and nowhere?
Let me seek Him, Let Him seek me.
Don't tell me He hates taverns,
a filth so filthy, and a harlot.
Don't tell me He loves hermits,
a man sacrificial, and a cult.
What if I say He is devoid of dependable sentiments?
Let me love Him, Let Him love me.
Don't guide me to recite holy books,
and that He restrains cuss words.
Don't tell me His prayers are important,
more than the chirping and croons of birds.
What if I say He trusts my voice?
Let me call Him, Let Him call me.
Don't tell me He plays flute,
and a dervish would tell me His appearance.
Don't tell me He resembles joy and not melancholy,
and that Good Gracious was a human once.
What if I say He is what you see with the eyes; eyes not on your
face?
Let me make Him, Let Him make me.

22. A Letter From The Moon To The Sun

"The sun watches what I do, but the moon knows all my secrets."

-J.M. Wonderland

Dear Glower,
It's your boon that
I'm making this gloomy night silver,
by lightening the earth that has
plenty of seekers.
They're seeking light;
light to show 'em the right path to peace,
if not greatness of life.
I hope our duo keeps serving the needy;
you protect it from the shiver,
and I from the sweat.

23. The Heart Of A Woman

"A woman is the full circle. Within her is the power to create, nurture and transform."

-Diane Mariechild

It takes -
to heal a wounded,
to ice a burnt,
to strengthen a fragile,
to paint a black,
to replenish a withered,
to sail a broken ship,
to sweet a bitter,
to make a flower; nurture it, and
to lose oneself to resemble God -
the heart of a woman.

24. They Aren't Ready For Me Yet

I'm the sky;
the sky of thoughts in which
no bird other than mine
ever flew making them conclude
I never existed.
I'm the ocean;
an ocean of treasures in which
no one could dive, and
those who tried gave up on the surface,
concluding that I lacked depth.
But I existed.
But I had it, depth.
It's just they ain't ready for me yet.

25. A Love So Physical

"*I was not allowed a physical lover. Falling in love
with love was the best I could get.*"

-Lionel Blue

A LOVE SO PHYSICAL,
IS THRIVING IN THE AIR,
THAT BLINDFOLDS YOU TO UNSEE

THE TRUTH;
THE TRUTH IS CALLED THE LOVE OF LEGENDS.
IT FUELS BODIES TO CATCH EACH OTHER
BEFORE SOULS DO,
AND SAYING 'I LOVE YOU' WAS NEVER EASIER.
TRUST ME,
LOVE WAS NEVER SO CORRUPTED,
AND WHEN I SAY 'SO' HERE,
I SAY IT AT THE TOP OF MY VOICE.

26. My Love So Inevitable

Even if I weren't here,

my love for you would have been.
It seems
as inevitable as death;
it had to occur.
It is in the moment, and
will be in all the morrows we have for this life.
And I know one day,
I will shed off
like leaves of November,
but this love that I've planted for you
will grow only.

27. Somewhere Away from The City Of Concrete

*"I took a walk in the woods and came out taller than
the trees."*

-Henry David Thoreau

When the brown leaves,
short of water,
get mashed under my boots,
a clutter produces, and
a current of air whistles
to give it good background music.
Hard to stop,
my soul goes out and
explores the small and big branches of the trees;
big trees making the grass shady.
Green that I find in the woods,
is healer and break,
to my wounded and wandering soul;
the soul that is brainwashed,
by the city of concrete.

28. I Am The Old Rose

"Love and a red rose can't be hid."

-Thomas Holcroft

Oh, love,
I'm the old rose,
haven in your least favorite book.
You'll never hold me again, and
I'll be stuck on the same page,
to wither me for years.
But the day,
you will open the book,
accidentally,
I'll smell the same for you,
even if it's gonna be
for a fleeting moment.
I promise,
I'll never enter your story again.
Neighbor books on your bookshelf,
will keep telling me,
if you're doing well. and
I'll happily picturise you,
reading a love story,
setting your hair strand
behind your ear.

29. The Abandoned Star

"They say that abandonment is a wound that never heals. I say only that an abandoned child never forgets."

-Mario Balotelli

On one chilled winter nightfall,
while scrolling in my corridor,
with a head whirlpool of feelings,
this one star captured my eye.
In the black-blue sky,
it appeared abandoned,
as there were no other stars.
Still,
it was twinkling its best.
The sharp wind,
that cooled my nose tip,
made a serene sound in my ears.
A tear rolled down my eye,
and I don't know why,
I felt I was watching the mirror,
when I was watching the star.

30. Where One Attains Oneness

"*The body has many needs. But the soul has only one:
To be with God.*"

-Yasmin Mogahed

Dear,
Energies so mystic!
Now and here,
in this moment,
I surrender my vagabond soul to thy ways.
Guide it to the amber,
or to the doom.
Just say;
say to me what's needed to be said.
I'm all ears.
Give me eyes for I can see
whence are you coming,
to take me away to the world;
the world where
one attains Oneness.

About The Author

Coming from the small town of Haryana - Narnaul, Harsh Sharma is the proud son of Mr. Krishan Kant Sharma and Mrs. Sudesh Sharma. He considers writing his lifeline. Incognito here and lost in a more beautiful world, this chap has co-authored 10+ anthologies including one national-level anthology named Coming of age by Split poetry India and one record book anthology named Those 48 hours. He has also compiled his anthology with 55 writers from all over the India, USA, and China named Melting Hearts. Recently, he has been honored with the Spectrum budding writer award, 2021 in literature by an organization registered under MSME (Ministry of micro, small and medium enterprises). His debut novel "The Story Of Three Voids" is winning hearts. Harsh believes that where there is sophistication, there is always kindness hidden. Enthusiast enough to imagine aspired enough to write - seems his personality inked in words. Despite being a writer, he aspires to influence social media at his best. His introverted nature boosts his tendency to observe and write better than before. To know more about him, Follow him on

Instagram: @author_harsharma and @an_aspired_pen

or write to him at sharmaharsh24122000@gmail.com

By The Same Author

"If you want to save someone, that's sympathy. If you need to save someone, that's love.' Residing in humid Lucknow, Bhuvik is trying to forget the love of his life. His incomplete love story pierces his heart every time nostalgia hits him. One day, from out of the blue, little Aadya enters his life only to make it a more complex riddle. The girl's acknowledgment of pain is way too ahead of her age. What heaviness that little heart carries? Roshani, a happy-go-lucky lady, has found her solace in her own made world with Aadya. She seems full of life and pretends that everything is perfect. But is life ever perfect? When God was created, he knew no perfection. So he left a void in everyone, may it be physical or mental or by birth or written in destiny. That void eats us until someone comes and fills it with their love and devotion. Everything falls into the right place and your heart says, 'yes! This is the one!' The three protagonists of the saga are no different. Will they find their lost pieces in each other or fate has something heartbreaking for them on its list? 'THE STORY OF THREE VOIDS' by Harsh Sharma will ride you on the roller coaster of emotions and is a perfect example of how words can change life."

Praises For Author's Previous Work

"A truly enchanting read, worth your time."

-Mini Balakrishnan (Author of "Dare to live")

"The story gives a substance of life, and how we move around looking for affection and strong sentiments."

-Arnav (Book reviewer)

"I'll recommend you to hold on with the story and discover yourself."

-Tanmay Mehta (Book Reviewer)

"The story gives an essence of life, and how we move around in search of love and supportive feelings."

-Sansriti Pandey (Book Reviewer)

"The tale moves from one character to the next flawlessly and smoothly."

-Prabal Tandon (Book Reviewer)